WINNIPEG

D0384910

WITHDRAWN

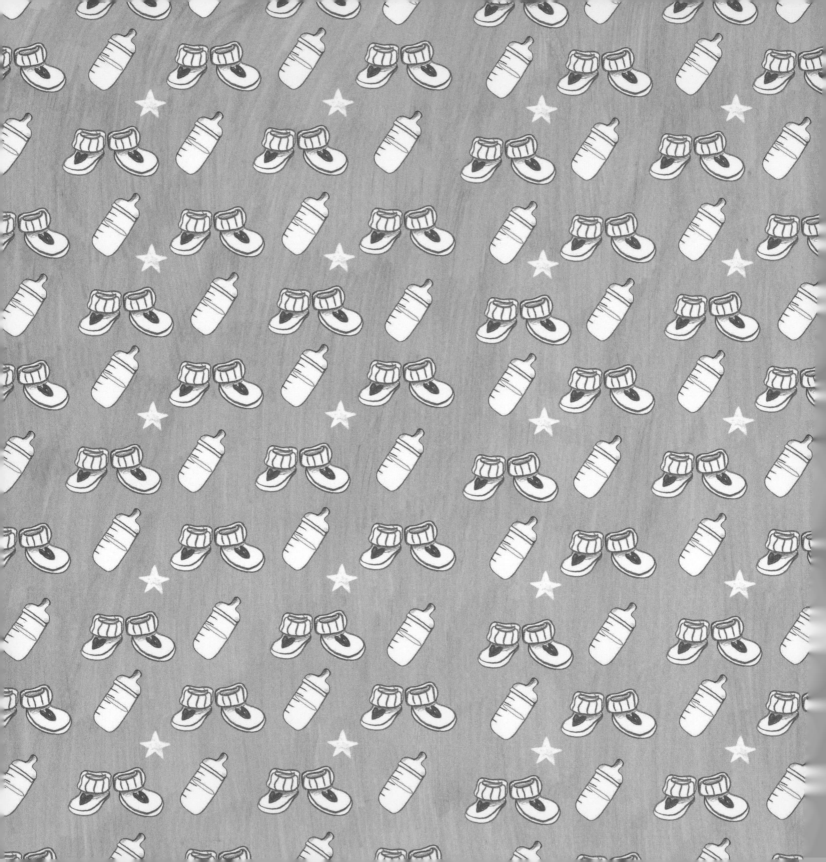

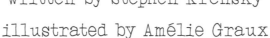

We Just Had a Baby

written by Stephen Krensky

illustrated by Amélie Graux

CAPSTONE YOUNG READERS
a capstone imprint

Published by Capstone Young Readers,
a Capstone Imprint
1710 Roe Crest Drive
North Mankato, Minnesota 56003
www.mycapstone.com

Text copyright © 2016 Stephen Krensky
Illustrations copyright © 2016 Capstone Young Readers

All rights reserved. No part of this publication may be reproduced in
whole or in part, or stored in a retrieval system, or transmitted in any
form or by any means, electronic, mechanical, photocopying, recording,
or otherwise, without written permission of the publisher. For information
regarding permissions, write to Capstone Young Readers,
1710 Roe Crest Drive, North Mankato, MN 56003.

Library of Congress Cataloging-in-Publication data is available
on the Library of Congress website.

Summary: A young boy gets a new baby sister and must learn how to adjust.

ISBN: 978-1-62370-603-6 (hardcover)
ISBN: 978-1-62370-604-3 (eBook)

Designer: Aruna Rangarajan

Printed and bound in China.
092015   009209S16

For Andrew and Nicole,
who both came first.
—S.K.

Pour Rachid, mon amour,
pour nos futurs petits choux.
—Amélie

We just had a baby.
It wasn't my idea.

She took a while to get here.
We waited and waited.

It seemed to take forever.

And after all that waiting,
there she was.

I thought she
would be bigger.

The baby blinks and wiggles.
Everyone thinks
this is amazing.

When I blink and wiggle,
nobody even notices.

We both have ten fingers
and ten toes. I counted
to make sure.

Mine are bigger.

The baby wears
a diaper. She doesn't
know what else to do.

I am way ahead of her.

The baby grabs my finger.
She holds on tight.

I guess she likes me.

The baby just drinks milk.
No pizza. No ice cream.

Too bad for baby!

The baby takes
a bath every day.
She is learning
how to splash.

I'm a good teacher.

The baby makes noises.
She giggles and coos
and burps.

And she cries. A lot. That's what she does best.

Now the baby rolls over.
But she doesn't roll back —
even after I showed her how!

The baby likes to play peek-a-boo.
But I have to do all the work.

When I smile
at the baby, the
baby smiles back.

When I frown
at the baby, the
baby looks scared.

I try to smile most of the time.

I'm glad the baby
keeps trying new things.
I hope she grows up soon.

I have BIG plans
for us!

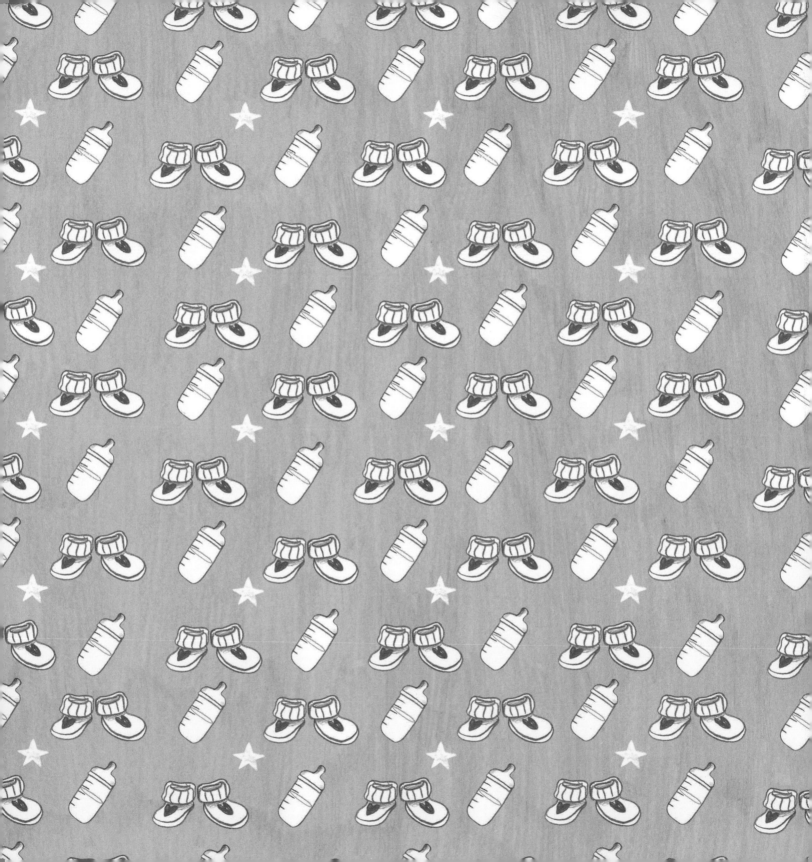

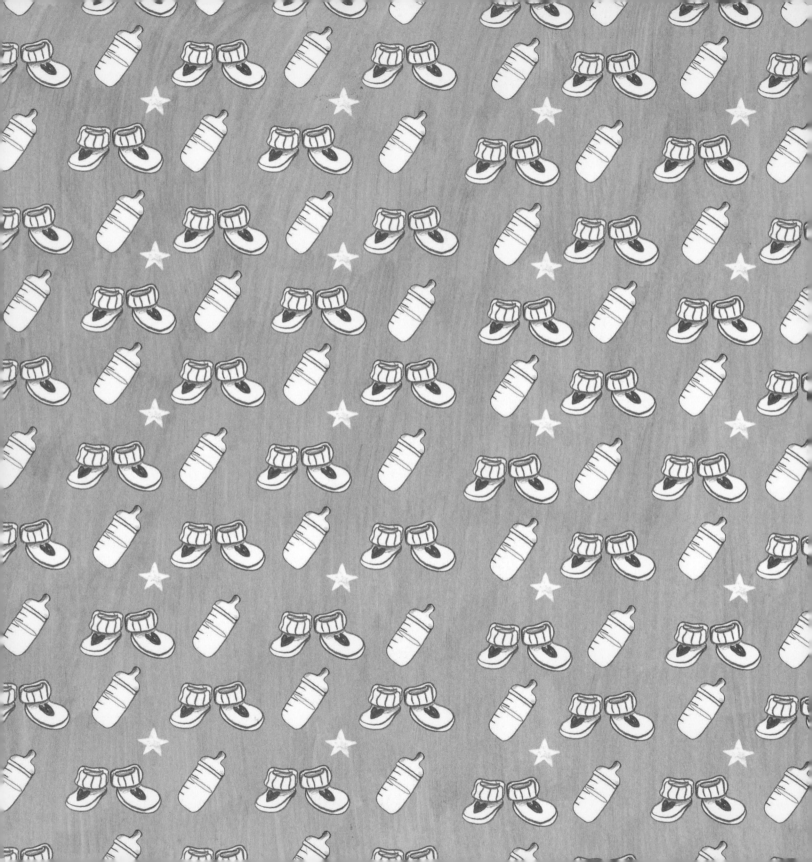